AN ORANGE,

A SYLLABLE

ALSO BY GILLIAN SZE

POETRY

Fish Bones
The Anatomy of Clay
Peeling Rambutan
Redrafting Winter
Panicle
Quiet Night Think

∎

PICTURE BOOKS

The Night Is Deep and Wide
My Love for You Is Always
You Are My Favorite Color
When Sunlight Tiptoes
The Little Green Envelope
I Drew a Heart

AN ORANGE,
A SYLLABLE

gillian sze

Copyright © Gillian Sze, 2025

Published by ECW Press
665 Gerrard Street East
Toronto, Ontario, Canada M4M 1Y2
416-694-3348 / info@ecwpress.com

All rights reserved. No part of this publication may be reproduced, stored in a retrieval system, or transmitted in any form by any process — electronic, mechanical, photocopying, recording, or otherwise — without the prior written permission of the copyright owners and ECW Press. The scanning, uploading, and distribution of this book via the internet or via any other means without the permission of the publisher is illegal and punishable by law. This book may not be used for text and data mining, AI training, and similar technologies. Please purchase only authorized electronic editions, and do not participate in or encourage electronic piracy of copyrighted materials. Your support of the author's rights is appreciated.

Editor for the Press: Michael Holmes /
a misFit Book
Copy editor: Emily Schultz
Cover photograph: "White Curtain" by Jonathan Borba. Used under Unsplash License.
Cover design: Jessica Albert

LIBRARY AND ARCHIVES CANADA CATALOGUING
IN PUBLICATION

Title: An orange, a syllable / Gillian Sze.

Names: Sze, Gillian, 1985- author

Identifiers: Canadiana (print) 20250223627 | Canadiana (ebook) 20250223635

ISBN 978-1-77041-851-6 (softcover)
ISBN 978-1-77852-504-9 (ePub)
ISBN 978-1-77852-505-6 (PDF)

Subjects: LCGFT: Poetry.

Classification: LCC PS8637.Z425 O73 2025 | DDC C811/.54—dc23

This book is funded in part by the Government of Canada. *Ce livre est financé en partie par le gouvernement du Canada.* We acknowledge the support of the Canada Council for the Arts. *Nous remercions le Conseil des arts du Canada de son soutien.* We would like to acknowledge the funding support of the Ontario Arts Council (OAC) and the Government of Ontario for their support. We also acknowledge the support of the Government of Ontario through the Ontario Book Publishing Tax Credit, and through Ontario Creates.

PRINTED AND BOUND IN CANADA

PRINTING: COACH HOUSE   5 4 3 2 1

ECW Press is a proudly independent, Canadian-owned book publisher. Find out how we make our books better at ecwpress.com/about-our-books.

The interior of this book is printed on Sustana Opaque™, which is made from 30% recycled fibres and processed chlorine-free.

for A & E, forever

for M, always

Watch the sun until it becomes square.

—Yoko Ono

■

night fits   and I imagine myself held together in the dark
     solid as an embrace   I rest in a pit where sleep   kneels
nearer   night   is when I believe I can get to that
point where   it is possible   to pierce the page and show you
     the holes   when we think of a hollow   we picture
the empty space   even the word forces   my tongue to
cradle and soothe   a ball of air   *hello*   something says
hollow   I say in return   the next morning   just the metallic
drag   of a drawn curtain

I saw those first nicks of light when I was staring into the child's mouth as she cried. A newborn's cry begins softly, picking up in volume and panic. Without words, I scrambled to decipher her cries, her needs. (Who performed the world's first act of translation? *A mother*, says Mary Ruefle.) If I didn't tend to the child quickly enough, her cry would scale its peak: a wide *o* letting out a fine strand of breath. Small body puce and stiff with fury. Silence would stream from her and wrap me up in my own nerves. In that fit, I resided *inside* her mouth. A delicate primordial space where not even the radicals of words could be heard.

How to measure one's mouth by its words? We speak and speak, natter on, as early as our desires can be expressed. How many conversations, arguments, discussions, and persuasions occur since then? Witnessing the first words of the child, how to enumerate all the other words to come? The measure and value of their utterances. Speech that was in earshot and speech that was not. Silence threatening to spill over the rim.

The earliest Chinese pictograph found on oracle bones of the word *mouth* was a semi-circle with a line through it. It appears to be an open-mouthed smile. It evolved and in modern Chinese, the word "mouth"/*kou* (口) is now written as a square.

So I divided my page into squares. Among its many meanings, *kou* refers to both *entrance* and *exit*—fitting on those days when the child's wails patterned themselves on the intake and outtake of air and sound and air and sound. Encased, I wished only for a single thought to fill the space and make a square that came out even on all sides.

When the child started to speak, she would practise a word over and over. Repetition was not for perfecting enunciation; rather, she was overjoyed at finding a word for the thing. Each word a car, circling mysteriously through her mind. I started to record the appearance of words as she spoke them, each hitched along at random. Eventually, this record I kept fell behind and every time she opened her mouth, I could feel her speed through a dark tunnel without me.

Our first night together, you recounted your favourite story about Krishna. When he was a child, Krishna was tasked with collecting the fruit his friends plucked from a tree. Beneath the branches, he instead ate the fruit, one by one. Aggrieved, his friends accused him of eating dirt and so informed his mother. She scolded Krishna, who insisted that he didn't, even inviting her to look to be certain. She told him to open wide and when he did, she peered inside to discover not earth but the entire universe in his mouth. The total chaos of all existence encountered in one second. A vast speechlessness quilting her close.

My comparison of language acquisition to some train, some countable linearity, is embarrassingly wrong. Baby language, I soon found out, was catachrestic. The child's speech laid bare associations and accidents. In the tub, she would point to the eye of the toy whale and say, *Moon*. She would clamber up the stepstool and say, *Tree*. And when the child pointed to the cracks in the floorboards, she would say, *Hole*, followed by, *Ow*. Point to the hole in my sock and say, *Hole*. *Ow*. Point to the circles in the rug and say, *Hole*. *Ow*. All was lace. From the child's small mouth, she undid the world around me.

One spring you brought me flowers. A bouquet of lilies, most of which were still closed. I retrieved a vase from the cupboard. You brought me flowers and I placed them in the middle of the table. You sat on one end and I on the other. We watched them open. Each day we would sit there, just you, me, and the lilies. You brought me flowers and we noticed that the lily bulbs on my side of the vase were opening. You told me that they wanted to mate. You called this love. Their bright mouths gaped wide in my direction.

(It was a moment of weakness when you made words into poetry. Lilies don't love. Bees and hummingbirds don't pollinate because of desire. But we all know that feeling. That sense when you're in the grocery store, and you pick up something that plunges sweetly into the stomach. Or maybe from across a loud room, a pair of eyes belonging to the right face, a song, an object plucked from your dreams. You think, *Ah. This is the one.* You knew always to make the distinction between instinct and intellect, animal and subject. *Who are you?* you asked me. The accusatory *you*, which we both volleyed. *You, you, you.* A sort of coo snug in the mouth.)

Dougong is an ancient Chinese method of interlocking wood. Watchtowers and temples and dynasties have been built completely without bolts, screws, or nails. All the wooden parts—beams, brackets, pillars—fit with precise carpentry. A dialogue, too, is putting a picture together, closing all the gaps. When one speaks and the other replies, words snap together. Meanings are understood and there is a satisfying "click."

You read that and laugh. *That never happens,* you say. I know that and yet I wrote it. You and I know it's never one to one. How idealistic. How impossible. Words are always hungry for that fullness of sense, a phenomenon Simic describes as *impoverishments, splendid poverties.* When we find a way to speak to each other, our eyes look past, over the other's shoulders. We whisper over the inescapable breach.

I observe you through a door. For a time, it was porous between us. You weren't even sieved through. There was a wholeness that would come to me that I could gorge upon entirely. Some plum to wrap myself around. I write *gap* and think of the running highway that streams through the city. I picture two people standing on opposite sides, with nothing to look at but each other. The light is red and there is only waiting and waiting. Two people stare at each other, the windblown hair, the particular shoes, the shifting of weight. Desire flies between, striking errorful from the whizzing cars and trucks, finds itself urged by the light counting down the seconds before it is safe. Oh, how the curbs ache with potential.

The child repeats after me. You. *You*. Me. *Me*. Baby. *Baby*. Tautological play. A skipping rope between our hands, sweeping the air. I swing. The child swings. The arc falls high and low and high and low. Something true inserts itself into that space that the rope does not touch. You say, *How boring. The most useless moment in language.* You insist that there needs to be some chance that the statement is false. You are you. You are not you. If light is a fail-safe. If light means it is a conscious day.

The toy box is made of holes of varying shapes. The child's task is to take loose, colourful pieces and find the corresponding slots. A star. A crescent moon. A square. A circle. Shapes that have yet to fill with symbolic meaning. The child holds tight to sense, awkwardly takes pieces—often the wrong ones—and seeks the satisfying push that happens when things fit. Her attempts are numerous until she grows frustrated. She shrieks for me to help. I take the shape from her outstretched hand, find the hole, and only then does she hurriedly whack it through, the piece plonking into the box. It does not satisfy her. The child reaches for another shape. Her quiet determination cycles quickly to frustration. The box fills accordingly until there's nothing left. We empty it. We fill it again.

I try, one day, in earnest to count the child's words. I think I can put a number to the day, even for just an hour. I lose count quickly. *Tedious*, you say of my efforts. One day, you're standing across from me in a grocery store, approaching as I pick and bag apples, just to tell me I'm beautiful. Another day, you're silent, bagging your own apples. Every turn of the fruit to reveal a bruise. Every squeeze is just so.

Years before, I had taken a train alone to New York and visited MoMA. I watched Marina Abramović attempt to say every single word she could recall without repeating any of them. I could see words cluttered in her mind. She waded through the hoard, tossed each word out haphazardly, so they didn't even string sense. It was a prayer for the mad. The strain was obvious. The performance was called *Freeing the Memory*. It took her about ninety minutes before she cleansed herself of language and reached a velvet silence.

In our silence, I gathered words. Recalled middle of the night shouts, the words exchanged that became our own night, private and terrible. Our once wooing words became words misquoted, words sabotaged, words held hostage and again, always again, misunderstood. Lu Ji says, *A writer knocks on silence to make a sound.* And so in the silence, I gathered words as the night gathers stars, as swiftly as the day gathers each ray, and a suitcase gathers the clothes which will then gather the body in its loneliness.

■

I grid the page and step into the square of the day. The calendar on the wall enforces sameness. The slice of bread. The window that receives the waking light. The baby plate with a smiling hippo in the centre. I turn the bend at this meal, that meal, this hour, that one. Night arrives at an angle; I step over the line into the square of the next day.

My place is held by a small piece of felt that the child cut, deemed unusable, and left on the floor. I pick it up and bookmark the day, the hour and minute of being in the home. Another colour wash. Another roam of a vacuum. Another fit to quell. Another nap for the child to sink into. Then I go to the kitchen and wash the rice. Swirl the clouds that bloom again with each draining and rinsing. The word for hulled rice (米 *bí*) transforms once the rice is cooked (飯 *pn̄g*). The word is as much as its thing. As I rinse and re-rinse, I have time to realize this correctness of names. The sweet vapours rise just as the cooker pops *done* and all the meaning changes.

What is out there? I think I have forgotten. My world thickens down to the sweetness in each fold of laundry. The growing tower of cotton, tidy and eversteady. For a while, I can stop thinking and let the hands spread across the sleeves, the hems, the stitches. The hands know where smoothness is right, know where to put the parts and when the folds are finished. *We divide the clean from the dirty,* you told me. *There is only order and chaos.* Love leaps from the walls, lolls in the wreck. My hands knew (know) your own lines well. Marriages are dull—what did Virginia say to Vita over dinner? *Love makes everyone a bore.* We believed us to be simple, but even in every misunderstanding I could hear that opening line: *I am a little world made cunningly.* A scent of sleepy lavender. The many folds of vacant laundry purple forward.

The child's shirt is inside out. The cotton twirls into the most inelegant Möbius strip. Sleeves dangle uselessly. The child fits herself in anywhere and briefly wraps herself in eternity. I watch her feel out the wrongness around her middle. She considers it then shimmies the impossible shape off. She tries to stretch the shirt into its normal dimensions by tugging the middle. I interrupt her quiet to tell her to grip onto an edge, to follow the line. The world distills. In her hands, the unravelling. The child, the day, the moment forge through.

When the child was new and wound up in cries, you soothed her, called her a god. The medieval definition of God is a *necessarily existing being*. Who knew that the child's sound could fill up each crevice with such celerity. In my mind, the child grows, busts the windows with the soft rolls of her wrists and ankles. My home brims with child. When I look up, she blocks out the sky. Anselm's actual wording is that God is "that than which nothing greater can be conceived." When I wake to the word, the child is in my arms again, small again, and still crying.

One early morning, I took the child and stood at the threshold. From the front door I watched a woman call out from her balcony. *Goodbye.* A man looked back to wave as he ran across the street to his car. I witnessed their night just finishing. They broke into their day, each getting on separately. One to don her clothes, another down the street to some mysterious elsewhere. Each window a sonnet. Everything a perhaps. The window was left open, its emptiness deeply familiar.

我想你 (*wǒ xiǎng nǐ*). In Chinese, *I miss you,* is straightforward. At least it seems. Three characters, one for each English word. But "to miss" is a slippery verb. In Chinese, *xiang* is associated with other verbs so *I miss you* is also wrapped in *I want you / I think you / I believe you / I wish you / I suppose you / I feel like doing you / I would like you.* The word's heap holds us under.

This is my favourite encounter—of which there are many—with translation and its loss. It involves Flaubert, a broken glass, and you. I had a copy of *Madame Bovary*, a yellowed paperback translation. We found it together one day at a used bookstore. I started reading it that afternoon. Every page was sombre. Everything in the novel dramatic and full of pathos, phrases like, "stale gusts of dreariness." In that time, you had your own phrases. You used to say things to me like, *Look at how the flowers open. It's like they're in love with you.* And not a hint of irony. I got through one half of the novel before I misplaced the book. The last tumbler of the set I bought you for Christmas broke and I was the one to retrieve shards from the bottom of the sink. It felt inevitable, given your sudden absence. Shortly, after you'd gone, I found a modern translation of *Madame Bovary* and picked up where I left off. Tones shifted. The second half of the book was suddenly arch. Everything after that interruption unanticipated. To this day, I don't quite know how to feel about the book.

(Years later, I tell this story about reading *Madame Bovary* to a writer. I want my Flaubert to be left fragmented, but she cannot let it be. She stops up the holes. She says firmly, *Flaubert is not funny. Oh, I know—I have read the original. Flaubert is not funny.*

Then I recount this conversation, relay her words about my misreading of Flaubert's words over to you.

Well, Madame Bovary dies horribly in the second half. Followed by her husband. And her child has to work in a cotton mill. So maybe "corrosively satirical" or something like that?

You really should reread the book.)

A woman goes up on stage to accept an award. The lights shine down and she looks out into the audience. She has her speech memorized. She thanks, most of all, her *beloved*. I think of the word, uttered from her mouth for everyone to hear. It embarrasses me. I hear the word, but I drop my head in attempt not to see it and therefore not hear it. But the sound of it wafts towards me. It is not a word meant for me, but it rouges the air. I wonder, *Who uses that word so purposefully nowadays?* Her love floods its dark letters, overflows with significance.

Beloved. The past participle from the obsolete verb *belove*. To belove: "to please." But also, I discover, "to be pleased with." What is it like to be in the middle of a word? It is like an open door. When the woman says *beloved*, I can feel love swing both into and out of the room.

The fit dims in increments like a failing light. Darker, everything makes sense. When you look like yourself again, shy and abashed, I am reminded of what Seneca said: *anger is temporary madness.* In a fit, we are in a square of our own making, the perfect right angles where our rage meets resentment. The lines that mark off the fit are impenetrable. We shoulder the walls like it could be a way out. The past is close to the surface, right beneath our feet, so we reach down and come up with handfuls of damage. *You have only to behold the expressions of those possessed by anger to know that they are insane.* When it is dark, it is also quiet and the home tries on its own to make sense. I probe each of your words to feel the sting of your fit, ludicrous now but still effective.

What were your words when the home was at a standstill? *My love is limited.* The last dish fell from a cupboard. At a talk about love, a scholar spoke about *agape*. I never considered the ordered and clean conditions of *agape*, the superior, transcendent, unconditional love. I did not know it. A light flickered somewhere. You once wrote something to me on a napkin from across the table. Your pencilled words tucked themselves into the pages of my book and, years later, I would recover the napkin. Words faded from the rub. Above: that fallen body that wouldn't break.

One summer, before the child, you left the country. From a distance, I wished to receive postcards. The sight of your words filling that small square as I retrieved the mail. The dives of your unintelligible writing. Instead, you returned from your excursion with a book of blank postcards. You thought yourself clever. This blankness, you insisted, was pure potential. I could write and imagine anything I wanted you to say. *Anything*, you repeated, like you were selling me land. I could be your words. You would have no need to be the writer. Briefly, I could picture you, over there, small and far. I could picture your thinking of me over breakfast. *Anything*, you said again. *Dangerous*, I replied. In 1759, Denis Diderot wrote to his lover Sophie Volland: *Wherever there will be nothing, read that I love you* . . .

As usual, nothing is ever good enough for you.

You could just have written something like that.

Diderot? Really?

And you'd only need to write it once—once for truer effect.

Some trees grow together and never touch. Side by side, they hoist for the sky. Their branches never traverse and entangle. Even leaves, ever accommodating, know where the neighbouring trees are and reach only so far. The space between canopies is known as *crown shyness*. If you look up, you'll see that trees fit together, adopting the lines of the other like puzzle pieces. Between them is space for the falling light. Bright borders where speech relays back and forth, leaf to leaf. Look up. The shyness of trees allows the sun to slip unthinkably between you and me.

I remember the time you said our love was anemic, that you wanted it *meatier*. I misunderstood. Thought you said *meteor*. A whole universe apart, often where we found ourselves then. Together, you, the child, and I met in a place between land and water, flesh and comets. We searched out and clutched *verre de mer* in our small grips.

(*Why verre de mer?* you ask me. Simply because I prefer *verre de mer* over *sea glass*. I think it's the rhyme, or maybe how the same thing in two languages have no sound in common. *Verre de mer* soaked in what I imagined to be the appalled blue light of stars.)

The child has her first fit. It takes place at the corner of busy streets. The fit stuns everyone off their humdrum pathways and it is hard not to admire the sounds, stomps, and pounding coming from the small body that refuses to use its feet. Those who have never tried to peel a squalling child from the ground stare, wavering between shock and pleasure. The fit eventually meets the shore of their judgement. The fit is virtuosic. It lazes on a plinth and holds everyone's gaze. The sheen is undeniable. A fit needs an audience. It wants, most of all, me. The fit peeks sideways, hunts for me in the crowd, locks in, demands that I never look away. I witness the fit, which I know, logically, is an outburst beyond the child's control. A morning glory spectacle. One fytte fits all. I witness the fit, but then no longer know if it is a performance for or from me.

(The books all say that fits are uncontrollable and nonsensical because the child is undeveloped. Blame their unmellowed cerebrums. I am reminded of the midwife who also tutted at our bodies, so poorly designed and incapable of pulsing out a whole antelope or elephant. Something that can stand on its own feet moments after that shuddering fall into the electric expanse of here. And us, so sadly human, so unwittingly vertical. Releasing an underripe creature, our openings ill-placed at the bottom, like an old piggy bank with a tired rubber plug.)

the fit is all   mouth   the mouth is a bird   the fit
chirps incessant and silver   the mouth fits   the mouth is
sacramental   the mouth is brightness   upon
brightness   the fit is blinding   the fit   and the mouth
are one   the mouth finds its fit   in the fytte   the mouth
always shapes itself to the fit   the mouth is embossed
the mouth   is boss   I think this will all fit   and the mouth
can only muster   *Maybe*

The child enjoys pushing her face into mine, jabs as if to break a surface. Utter joy as we collide. I see stars but she laughs and presses her forehead against me. I worry how she has hurt herself in her rapture. The bones in my face are tender by the end of the day. At night, I can't bear to see children on TV, to think one day the child will be older, speaking, playing, arguing, leaving. I tell you to change the channel. It is too much to think about. It reaches all the way inside. Lately when I cry, the child watches, an expression between delight and fear. There are words, stifled and entangled. The child unknots the sounds to see each glowing syllable. They mean nothing to her yet. Their sillage, an eternity spaced out in a few minutes.

Somewhere a poet is about to read his poem. He says to the audience: *This poem is about ripe cherries and summer.* A heavy pause before he continues. *So it's about sex.* The audience chuckles. As he reads his poem about cherries and heat, my mind turns to the time we sat on the stoop, spitting cherry pits into a silver bowl. The child was asleep. We had escaped to the steps where we drank beer and tongued the stones out with a *ping*. Across the street a squirrel tumbled from a branch. We just happened to be facing that way when we saw it land on the hot sidewalk. Red dripped from our chins. Inside a body of steady breaths. Outside the soft rag of another.

I think of this poet again in another place, a later time, when I think I have almost forgotten him. A canoe opens its mouth to the clouds, waits for rain. Mint hull on water. From here it's just a birthday cake floating on quiet glass. *This poem is about rain and boats. So it's about sex.* I am laughing at the poet, at his cherries, and the heat that prickled his skin. Before the rain comes, I ask if you really believe what he said that night when he was reading his poems. How much of reality leaks into the space of a poem? You simply say, *Poetry is about truth. Not fact.* (Later, much later when you have forgotten about the poet and the cherries and the rain, when I quote yourself to you, you say: *I sound like a pompous jackass.*) Leaves pit-pat past our legs. They rush towards the water, hurried and bold. When we walk away from the boat, from the water, it is just autumn pouring down between us.

The child cries because she cannot find her shadow. I tell the child to turn around and walk backwards. She is not satisfied. She wants the sun in her face and her shadow in front. If the child cannot see it, it is not there, and so she is not there. It is so plain. It is scary to be this small and suddenly alone to confront this dazzle. I try to explain how the sun topples the shadow backwards, so it's always where you once were and not where you are going. It must be scary to be this sudden. This dazzle is hers alone and scary. The child cannot look directly into the light and into the dark at the same time.

When the child sleeps, the whole house holds its breath. A drip. A tap on a somewhere window. The fridge's hum catches. A light bulb hangs out of tune. It is a slow coiling. When the child sleeps, the house doesn't belong to anyone. The child's first cry fills the room, then the stairwell. It is a house filling up. The cry seeks the bottom so it can know for certain where to begin. The floor bows and creaks its acceptance of upholding all this weight.

Cries whittle away the night. In the white muffled morning, I return to words and, to my bewilderment, nothing makes sense. I misread everything I have written. Vowels are warped into other sounds. Meaning flies on tendrils. The brightness barely scuffs the exhaustion. I open a notebook and when I read *agape* I mistake divine love for the mouth, *wide open in wonder.* The child grows. Feet, once plump and expressive, lengthen. They land on the ground, sure and strong. No more are the buoyant cheeks, which suddenly betray a soft jawline, a sensual rune. Hair grows out its downy fineness. Teeth pop out, nearly audible in their abruptness. The round weight is replaced with bone angles and knitted stretch. And this is not even peculiar in the slightest. It is when the child speaks, first a sentence of sound and next a sentence of clear meaning. Sea-formed words foam forth and settle between us.

Nothing is safe when the trees are sharpened by the winter wind. Neither swallows nor black-capped chickadees nor cardinals. Nothing can survive those mangled spokes, now stripped of their softness. An empty garbage bag lifts off for the treetops. It snags, shapes its blackness to every gust. Inflating, slackening, and then braving the white skies. It pulls and pulls but can't let go. Meanwhile the days shiver earthward. Birds don't dive so much as swoon from roof to roof. Their wings open and lock. For a second, birds appear as paper cut-outs. I expect them to succumb to their own flatness and reveal the usual chaotic rise and flutter. Sheets and sheets of juncos that turn around and against the wind. Everything is planar: wingspan against blue ether, time against space. At the last minute, their wings wink alive in unison. Birds are animated from shadows in that interlude between going and arriving.

the fit is its own   sad   pale animal   the fit   is the
soothing burn in the belly   after the swallow   the fit dares us
the fit luxuriates   in its spleen   the fit   has no need for
          words and   true meanings   the fit   has no need for
true   the fit   begins with   me the fit   becomes us
so we share it   the fit   wants us   to choke on it   the fit
wants us   to break our   natural patterns   the fit   wants
us   to break   the fit   hems us in   like a square the fit
finds us   yearning   the fit does not care about
     tomorrow   the fit   wants so badly to be   trendy
the fit   will promise   that this is the last time and we will believe it
          when it slinks through the bars of the square
          through the shallow grins   of the   night

∎

An orange, halved. *This is for you.* The child eats each half like a whole thing. Disregards each pocket crescent. The child does not care. It's all the same. All just orange. Even the word in her mouth is all one thing, each syllable an indiscernible wave. The *r* isn't obvious or heard but it's all orange in the word and in the pulp mashed between the teeth. What's left drips through fingers. Citrus in the air. The echo of a peel.

The child adds -*ed* to actions. She does so to indicate something that has passed (*bring, bringed*). She is right in theory, but most of the time she is wrong. You correct her every time. *It's a strong verb,* you instruct. *Hold. Held. Write. Wrote.* You sigh. *Language accommodates the lazy,* you once said when I got it wrong. And speakers are lazy by nature. I cannot blame the child for choosing efficiency. The verb slipping into the past with the smallest addition of sounds, consistent and predictable. I never correct her. *Write. Writed.* Why must the grammar strengthen if it already works? *It's a weak verb, so it's correct,* I overhear you say. *Love. Loved.*

I know that I can't stay inside forever. Eventually everything has to go. You take the child and walk through the door. It is a gesture so simple: feet taking their places, one after the other. And yet I stand on the other side, puttering about, checking to see if the stove is off, the windows closed, the faucets tight. I worry the house will explode in our absence, *Though that is better than in our presence,* you offer. I change pants. These legs in those holes. Or maybe not. These feet in these shoes. You and the child watch me. The house is cool. The open door and its straight lines swing past the threshold. It is one step to cross over, into the light and the heat, but until then it is impossible. Since the child's arrival, even the most basic task has become jagged with nerves. I am afraid of getting trampled by the space separating us. I am earnest when I tell you that. So you and the child wait. I stare past you both and think, *Spindrift.* We all wait.

(You look it up. There is indeed a phobia of thresholds. The first search result is a forum where a man says that his first encounter with this phobia was with his dog. *My dog had it,* he wrote. *It was a sign that he had a brain tumour.* The exact diagnosis is: *Schwellenangst. The Germans have a word for everything,* you approve.)

Remember that morning—*did this even happen?* The moon pulsed the same light as the streetlights. The geese pecked at the grass, strolled the shore with those backward knees. When they drifted off, they left silver streaks behind them in the lake. Together the sky and lake cushioned a line of trees and clasped the last of autumn. When the sun lifted its head, the water stilled, unfurled like a petal, pink and smooth. The geese came out to sunbathe on the grass. They didn't dare touch the water alloyed from the November sun. *Where did you go?* I stared out with the child; the path between us and the lake, us and the geese, a trodden line of symmetry.

Finally outside, I join the child, who colours in a misshapen heart with chalk. The chalk breaks as she jabs at the pores in the concrete. What she wants is uniformity. The child doesn't know what dissatisfies her most: the misshapen heart, the holes left behind on the surface, or the broken bits at her feet. The child loses interest and leaves to pluck samaras off the grass. She tosses them just high enough so we can see them whirl briefly before they hit the ground. She does this again and again. She is happy once more. One day, smaller, the child tried to grab a toy while holding two others in her hands. How frustrating it was to fail. I had to explain that to hold something, you must let go of whatever is already there. I repeat this to the child, who must learn and relearn. Always for other things. Always in the same way.

It is the *and* that I notice. It is the *and, and, and* that surprises me most. The invisible crumb. The *ands* are tense mysteries. It is not a word like *sit*. It is not a word like *dance*. Or *purple*. Or *cracker*. It is not *ding-ding*, the child's word for *light*. It is that the child is suddenly aware that the conjunction is where things meet. And it is a chain of *ands*, a chain of that which moves, that which can be seen and tasted together. The child graduates from verbs and things. I realize the *and* is her sudden capacity to join the world without me.

The first snowfall and the child looks up. Our foreheads press together now against the window. Nowhere else to look but skyward. We try always to find that first point, the highest start. But we can see only where the streetlight shines. It's not snow we see, it's the instances of light. It's all too high, too dark to see where everything begins. So we throw our gaze up in dizzying repetition as each flake throws itself into this world. Between the two we can measure something that feels like *right now*, a forevering away of time.

Another night, another history: the sky showed signs of collapse. Small abjectless flakes. I told you I was afraid of black holes. You were amused by the distance between us and those unseeable things light years away. How fear still occupied the length that overtook even my own life. Who wouldn't be afraid of that which can reduce our globe to a pea? An unimaginable density palmed, purloined. You and I circled each other then, love like the darkest surface. Languid before the lance. We did it for years even when we hated the other. *Leave*, one would say. *Go*, the other replied. What kept us pinioned to the dark? What gravity? Black holes can come in pairs, the scientists discover. Between the distance from here and the expanding cosmos, what is in fact two looks like one. The pull of one hole on the other prevents the other from havering. The need is in balance. The illusion is pulled tight to perfection.

■

A whole manuscript of poems appears on the screen in a sequence of squares. The file's corrupt. *Sense has dissolved,* is all I can think as I surrender to this loss. All around me squares—bathroom tiles, Post-its, napkins, picture frames, baby bibs—each prop my steps, my movements.

Kazimir Malevich's famous *Black Square* was deemed the "zero point of painting." How do we begin? Here, with nothingness. Stare so it aches to look. The invisible scaffolding. *Zero*: where, according to Malevich, "the true movement of being begins." The black void could be anything and after it was complete it became, quite possibly, everything.

Later, historians discover that beneath the black paint was movement muffled. A racist phrase that some attribute to Malevich, some not. They discover another painting, one more colourful and complex. Patches of primary colours that emerge like the stained glass of a church. I look closely at the painting and its craquelure. The fine white webbing says: too much paint, too much black, too much nothing. I turn to you, disappointed. *Everything is falling apart,* I say. *Everything has already been falling apart,* you correct me.

All leaps imperfectly. (*I sound like a pedantic prick,* you say when I record and repeat your words.) There are gaps in what we see, and we aren't conscious of how much we scorn it. Not even a chance to say, *Oh!* Our brains save us this trouble and grip onto the edges to fill in the rest. Assume texture. Imagine the sun, dappled. Imagine the brume that cuts across the path. All those mystery spots where there is nothing. The mind would rather sneak behind, fill it in for you, convince you that something is truly there. The child sits in the tub, cups the water to her face, comes up dry. *Where did it go?*

Josef Albers painted hundreds of squares from 1950 onwards. To him, the square was order, elegance, beauty at its simplest. In *Homage to the Square*, he paints a shrub-green square nestled in a grey square nestled in another grey square. A matryoshka of squares. He painted a series of these squares for twenty-five years. Why the squares, again and again, in the same arrangement? His answer: *Because I do not see that there is, in any visual articulation, one final solution.* Did he know that even Kazimir Malevich's *Black Square* doesn't measure up to a perfect square because it was made freehand? That it's not even black, but a mixture of non-black colours? When the child has a fit, I am convinced that it is all one singular violent expression. The solid black of incoherence and anger. I harden against her fit. When I soften, the fit crackles open, recedes. The beguiling peach of exposure, whipping bright the holy dark.

One good picture with ten holes in it is better than ten bad pictures with no holes, so Edvard Munch says. He paints the best fit I know in *The Scream.* The whole landscape an arrhythmia of inside colours. The petrified holes of the face. *You want and want and want,* you once said. *Who ever gets everything?*

What is enough then?

Sixty percent.

You had your moments with numbers. Munch's orangebitter sky reminds me of lilies. I remember how the raw blooms rushed their sweet fragrance, but even that, in time, becomes forgettable.

the fit is   coy   the fit knows it has gone too far   the fit
cries ~~for~~ by itself   light appeared and the grey sky was
still there utterly complete   the fit admitted it didn't come seeking
omens   and yet the fit found a leaf in the shape of itself
the fit found all of the lost suchness of things   it found the
knot in the wood   peered through and saw itself

What does it mean to square something? It is to multiply oneself with itself. A more than doubling. A more than mirroring. I see our hands take the clay and mould something out of something. What forms breaks down again and it is all our doing. We repeat, reshaping and destroying, always starting from the bottom. I wonder if this is what it's usually like between two people. It is not the clay that multiplies, it is the new shape, the memory of past shapes, and all the air around. Look how the feelings square themselves. Look at the grudges. Little mathematician. Smooth logician. When I turn my back on you it's still you I see before me.

Piece by piece I erect a structure that piece by piece you take apart. You could always see the spaces, whipping straight my sentences and then snapping off each word into a jumble at our feet. *Together we accomplish nothing.* The energy of our exchange squandered until even words couldn't bear these acts of cancellation.

In 1953, Robert Rauschenberg asked Willem de Kooning for a drawing. After weeks of work by de Kooning, Rauschenberg took the sketch and erased it all. He framed the result and titled it: *Erased de Kooning Drawing*. A blank square of traces and fine-lined damage. But empty space tingles the desire to know. Fifty years later, the erased square went through an infrared scan to see more of what was no longer there. Turned out de Kooning had already taken an eraser to his work, so lines crossed over other lines, version over version. The conjured ghosts haunting over and around each other. In the enhanced image, you can see the rough lines of a squatting woman, positioned as if to give birth. And then she was gone.

■

Another fight, another footnote. These days everything between us is marginal. You once brought me postcards of Vilhelm Hammershøi's paintings, which I kept while trying to count words. Somewhere, sometime else, Jacques Derrida wrote on a postcard to his love, *I would like to write to you, so simply, so simply, so simply.* But all the postcards you handed to me were blank. Just image after image of Hammershøi's apartment interiors. I think of the peace and stillness that permeate his paint. The sallow light. The straight lines that run and fork to create doors and windows. Without the presence of someone, the door becomes the main subject of the piece. A stoic character, both open and closed like a secret. I can't tell which. A woman stands in a room and becomes as inert as a table corner. You call her rage impotent but it streams through and lights up the whole space.

What spasms most in Hammershøi's interiors are those reaching spaces between open doors. Openings that fit me, a past me, a maybe me. The uncertain lines and ruts. A shadow swoons itself over a door. This light is conditional. The room says that there's no one there. *I have always thought there was such beauty about a room even though there weren't any people in it,* Hammershøi says, *perhaps precisely when there weren't any.* Lines blow open: a room into another room, into another. Light-stained entrances. The here and there of me.

Oh, all those backs. I know more of Hammershøi's wife, Ida, from behind, standing back here out of frame. Her back and the receding wall. Her back and a tureen. Her back and the unplayed piano. Her back and a brown desk. Her back draped in darkery. The sober light defines all the waiting, all the quiet. What does she read? What does she gaze upon on the street below? Is that letter even for her? When the light hits the floor, we know that it never moves again.

the light insofar   the light as   partition   the light's
weight   so different from yesterday   the light as chassis
     holding up this stillness   the light and its   liquids
and grooves   the light's implacable angles   the light's
     hollowness   the light's collapse   the light as empty
canvas   the light's impasto   the light   overharvested
and obedient   the light   speaks its own language
     we pass through its vocabulary   without fear

The austere walls awash with absence. There is no sign of the child in Hammershøi's rooms. No fingerprints or garish playthings. Not a trace of even a meal prepared, trailed, unswept. No air wracked with the clangour of a child, or the daily spats about who did what or who did not enough. No swelling of resentment to eclipse the shadows cast on the clean floor. I want to venture into the room alone without encumbering the dumbstruck atmosphere. Borrow, perhaps, the ease with which the light slices the air, defiant and hefty. Wherever I am, the child is. I can only look from a doorway that was never painted. I am diminished to an accent.

What can an artist do without leaving their home? Hammershøi painted over sixty works of the inside of his apartment: empty rooms—sometimes furnished, sometimes not. A piano. A desk. A table blocking the doorway. A chair facing a wall. He painted shadows and light, the feeling of emptiness. Lines, so many lines, reaching deep into the canvas. I imagine that the farther he moved forward with his brush, the more he paced backwards within himself.

If all of Hammershøi's paintings of the apartment were pieced together, the result would be akin to a hall of mirrors. Inconsistent dimensions, skewed slants, and varying depths render the entire interior of the home inaccurate. And yet taken apart, each painting carries its own perfect consonance. There is no sense of the warping dizziness of the whole when each interior is isolated. I am convinced that this is a lesson in beauty. Or love.

Femininity in that precious space between Ida's collar and her hairline. The neck unsuspecting. Open only to light and a fallen gaze. The neck receives everything. The brightest spot on the canvas, so raw in its smallness. How many times does one look at a lover and really see? His Ida, painted time and again in those rooms where they lived in solid light. Ida, often there, often gloomy, almost always from the back. Ida inside. Ida facing here and there. Ida receding. Ida in black. Ida with bent head. Ida with a dish. Ida beside two bottles resting on a cool table. Ida in my poem. *What means practically the most for me is the lines*, Hammershøi said in a rare interview about his interiors. What of the lines of Ida? To ask this is to see the back of her neck and divine a butterthick warmth.

My favourite painting of Ida is not the one where she is sitting on a chair point-blank facing the wall, or reading a letter, or sitting at the desk, or idle at the piano. My favourite painting of her is in that parlour where Hammershøi painted so many versions of what he saw: open doors, white doors, doors ajar, rooms beyond. Sometimes Ida is there. Sometimes she is not. If one were to see through his eyes, the succession of interior paintings would look like a comical stop animation, Ida bouncing around the rooms. In one interior, she is, as usual, seen from the back wearing her long black dress. One hand rests on the doorknob. She looks ready to walk through, and yet her head is turned to look at another open door on the adjacent wall. The twist of her body shows us a split desire. Her dress picks up the shadows. A sliver of light comes at odds, through a window two rooms away.

What did the painter want to hide? Some say that he just was never good at painting faces. Hammershøi was a quiet man and the words he could share to clarify this decision are now secret. So, I have no choice but to believe that this is an acceptable reason. I have no choice but to stare at all those backs.

What troubles Ida? In the rare painting where she is seen from the front, viewers remark on how dolorous she appears. Some say she yearned for the child that was never to be. Some say she suffered fits the way her own mother did. Maybe she is always seen from the back so this pain remains private.

She carries it in front of her. She holds it with no hands.

All the lines will spiral to a point. The cries will greet silence. The last wood piece will slot into place and become something to walk through or under. *And then the light,* Hammershøi says. *Naturally it also has a great deal to say.* So the brush sails across the final edge of the canvas.

It was a mathematician who used to sign off with a square at the end of a proof. He saw it first used in journals to mark the end of a story, so he borrowed it. In math, the typographical mark is called a tombstone, though it's also been called the *halmos*, after the mathematician. I don't have to tell you that I have lost count of words. (You were never one for final causes anyway.) So let me linger in these rooms, these mouths, I failed to fill. One moment I saw all the syllables, *precious alphabet,* full of meaning, cliffing around me. Then it shone out of you and the child, sharpened glints I could not refuse. It was just like stepping into a painting where a door opened to another room, and another door into another room. And at each turn, the light bent, never far behind. And when the mouth opens, naturally, it, too, has a great deal more to say.

ACKNOWLEDGEMENTS

My deepest gratitude to editors Michael Holmes and Emily Schultz for their generous and scrupulous reading of this manuscript. Thanks also to the team at ECW Press for their invaluable support. This book was written alongside many vital exchanges with Sofia Bohdanowicz, Stephanie Bolster, Miljana Cunta, Mary di Michele, Jane Malcolm, Sara O'Leary, and Kate Sterns—thank you. A special thanks to Judith Herz—I miss you very much.

I always find myself back here: immensely grateful to my love, Manish Sharma, for his friendship, patience, and brilliance. Aalok and Eider, my little universes: I knew from the outset that I could never capture in words the earliest and most singular notes of your existence, and I am okay with that.

REFERENCES ARE MADE TO THESE AUTHORS, ARTISTS, AND WORKS:

Abramovic, Marina. *Freeing the Memory.* 1975. Video. New York, MoMA.

Albers, Josef. *Homage to the Square: Oasis.* 1961. Oil on hardboard. Toronto, Art Gallery of Ontario.

Albers, Josef. "Oral History Interview with Josef Albers, 1968 June 22–July 5," interview by Sevim Fesci for the Archives of American Art.

Anselm. *St. Anselm's Proslogion.* University of Notre Dame Press, 1979.

Champion, Jean-Loup, Frank Claustrat, et al. *Hammershøi: Painter of Northern Light.* Rizzoli, 2023.

Derrida, Jacques. *The Post Card.* Trans. Alan Bass. The University of Chicago Press, 1987.

Diderot, Denis, quoted in Jacques Derrida, *Memoirs of the Blind: The Self Portrait and Other Ruins.* University of Chicago Press, 1993.

Donne, John. "Holy Sonnets: I am a little world made cunningly." Poetry Foundation. Accessed January 25, 2025. https://www.poetryfoundation.org/poems/44108/holy-sonnets-i-am-a-little-world-made-cunningly.

Flaubert, Gustave. *Madame Bovary.* 1857.

Hammershøi, Vilhelm. *Dust Motes Dancing in the Sunbeams.* 1900.

———. *The Four Rooms.* 1914.

———. *Interior.* 1899.

———. *Interior from Strandgade with Sunlight on the Floor.* 1901.

———. *Interior with a Reading Lady.* 1900.

———. *Interior with a Seated Woman.* 1910.

———. *Interior with Four Etchings.* 1904.

———. *Interior with Ida in a White Chair.* 1900.

———. *Interior with Ida Playing the Piano.* 1910.

———. *Interior with Piano and Woman in Black.* 1901.

———. *Interior with Stove.* 1909.

———. *Interior with Young Woman from Behind.* 1904.

—. *Interior, Woman at the Open Door.* 1905.
—. *Open Doors.* 1905.
—. *The Tall Windows.* 1913.
—. *White Doors.* 1899.
Hammershøi, Vilhelm, Felix Krämer, and Florian Illies. *Vilhelm Hammershøi: Silence.* Hauser & Wirth Publishers, 2024.
Januszczak, Waldemar. "Vilhelm Hammershøi—So Many Shades of Grey." July 13, 2008. https://waldemar.tv/2008/07/vilhelm-hammershoi-so-many-shades-of-grey.
Ji, Lu. "The Joy of Words." In *The Anchor Book of Chinese Poetry.* Edited by Tony Barnstone and Chou Ping. Penguin Random House, 2005.
Malevich, Kazimir. *Modern Art.* Vol. 1: 1870–1944. Edited by Hans Werner Holzwarth and Laszlo Taschen. Los Angeles: Taschen, 2011.
—. *Black Square.* 1915. Oil on canvas. Moscow, Tretyakov Gallery.
Munch, Edvard. *The Scream.* 1893. Oil, tempera, pastel, and crayon on cardboard. Oslo, The National Museum.
—. "Art and Nature." In *Manifesto: A Century of Isms.* Edited by Mary Ann Caws. University of Nebraska Press, 2000.
Ono, Yoko. "Sun Piece." In *Grapefruit: A Book of Instructions and Drawings by Yoko Ono,* with an introduction by John Lennon. Simon & Schuster, 2000. First published 1964 by Wunternaum Press.
Palin, Michael. "Michael Palin and the Mystery of Hammershøi." YouTube. July 24, 2015. Video, 58:51. https://www.youtube.com/watch?v=HNfBf39QxIc.
Plato. *Cratylus.*
Rauschenberg, Robert. *Erased de Kooning Drawing.* 1953. Traces of drawing media on paper with label and gilded frame. San Francisco Museum of Modern Art.
Rich, Adrienne. *An Atlas of The Difficult World.* W. W. Norton & Company, 1991.
Ruefle, Mary. *Madness, Rack, and Honey.* Wave Books, 2012.

Seneca. *Moral Essays.* Vol. 1. Translated by John W. Basore. The Loeb Classical Library. W. Heinemann, 1928–1935. Last modified October 27, 2015. https://www.stoics.com/seneca_essays_book_1.html.

Simic, Charles. *Wonderful Words, Silent Truth.* University of Michigan Press, 2004.

Vad, Poul. *Vilhelm Hammershøi and Danish Art at the Turn of the Century.* Panoply Books, 1992.

Woolf, Virginia, and Vita Sackville-West. *Love Letters.* Vintage Classics, 2021.